How to Resist Temptation

Nicky Gumbel

ISBN 978 1 905 887 33 0

Published by Alpha International, Holy Trinity Brompton,
Brompton Road, London, SW7 1JA, UK.

How to Resist Temptation

Ephesians

Nicky Gumbel

Alpha

Ephesians 6:10–17

Finally, be strong in the Lord and in his mighty power. Put on the full armour of God so that you can take your stand against the devil's schemes. For our struggle is not against flesh and blood, but against the rulers, against the authorities, against the powers of this dark world and against the spiritual forces of evil in the heavenly realms. Therefore put on the full armour of God, so that when the day of evil comes, you may be able to stand your ground, and after you have done everything, to stand. Stand firm then, with the belt of truth buckled around your waist, with the breastplate of righteousness in place, and with your feet fitted with the readiness that comes from the gospel of peace. In addition to all this, take up the shield of faith, with which you can extinguish all the flaming arrows of the evil one. Take the helmet of salvation and the sword of the Spirit, which is the word of God.

How to Resist Temptation

Preface

Temptation is one of the marks of being a Christian – if you are a human being in this world and you are a Christian, you will struggle with temptation. Jesus himself was tempted. The good news is that we, as Christians, have the power to change the world. In the first part of the book of Ephesians, Paul tells us that we have the same power that raised Jesus from the dead. We are 'seated with Christ'. The same incomparably great power that raised Jesus lives in us. Ephesians 2:6 says, 'And God raised us up with Christ and seated us with him in the heavenly realms in Christ Jesus…'. You and I sit in this place of victory.

When I asked Dr Graham Tomlin, the Dean of St Mellitus College, London, the question 'what is evil?', he replied:

> Evil is nothing in itself. It is destructive, but it cannot create. It twists what is already there. It is potent and real and very attractive, but it is nothing in itself, it's a purely destructive force.

So where does evil come from? We cannot blame everything on the devil. I heard of one man who used to do just that. He went to lunch with a friend and arrived thirty minutes late. He said, 'The devil was in my gear box'. How do we work out what is the devil, and what is just life? If somebody takes your parking space, is that the devil, or is that just life?

Father Raniero Cantalamessa, Preacher to the Papal Household, describes the 'triple alliance' of the world, the flesh and the devil, sometimes referred to as the 'unholy trinity'. Paul refers to each of these in Ephesians.

First, the term 'this world', meaning a society organised without reference to God, 'You followed the ways of this world' (Ephesians 2:2). Secondly, the flesh, '...gratifying the cravings of our sinful nature and following its desires and thoughts', and finally, the devil, '...the ruler of the kingdom of the air, the spirit who is now at work in those who are disobedient' (Ephesians 2:2).

Further, in Ephesians 6 he describes the spiritual forces of evil in the heavenly realms. We are fighting against more than mere flesh and blood. Father Raniero stresses that it would be a mistake to reduce the focus entirely to one personified enemy, the devil. Rather there are three things at play – the world, the flesh and the devil. The enemy is around us, within us and above us; it is a triple alliance.

This triple alliance aims to destroy, but any destruction begins with a simple foothold. With reference to anger, Paul writes, '... do not give the devil a foothold' (Ephesians 4:27), because in life, a foothold can easily become a stronghold. Although he refers primarily to an individual's anger, his instruction could easily refer to fear, jealousy, pride, self-hatred, unforgiveness, bitterness, or addiction to substance abuse, sex or gambling.

His instruction can apply to more than the individual. That is, it can be applied to 'rulers and authorities' – global evils. The twentieth century saw global evils on a massive scale: Nazism, personified in Hitler; vicious dictatorship, personified in Pol Pot. The twenty-first century faces other global problems: the huge spiritual hunger in the heart of every human being, the giant terrorist threat, AIDS, starvation on a scale unknown in human history, the destruction of the environment, and corrupt government in many nations.

Evil is not just out in the world; it is in us as well. Winning the battle against the enemy starts with us as individuals. Paul tells us how to win this battle. First of all, we have to take responsibility. It is so easy to blame others; our parents ('I'm like this because my parents were'), our genes ('I've always been like this') or our circumstances ('I would not be like this if it were not for this'). Paul says, 'Be strong in the Lord, and in his mighty power' (Ephesians 6:10). Rather than being passive we must do something; take *responsibility* and take *action*. Paul lists some of the good habits we need to cultivate to get rid of the bad.

1. Fix your eyes on Jesus

Focus on Jesus with:

' …the belt of truth buckled round your waist'
(Ephesians 6:14).

Truth means truth of character. One of the temptations we all face is to be insincere, to be the kind of person it suits us to be in a given situation, which is the opposite of integrity, authenticity and being real. Truth of character is being ourselves and living with integrity, transparency and sincerity. But, truth here also means truth of doctrine – biblical truth. Both truth of character and truth of doctrine are personified in Jesus. Jesus called himself 'the truth' (John 14:6). This is why the writer of Hebrews says that if we want 'to throw off everything that hinders and the sin that so easily entangles,' we must 'fix our eyes on Jesus' (Hebrews 12:1–2).

Satan is described as a liar, and the father of lies. What is the lie? John tells us in his gospel that the liar is whoever denies that Jesus is the Christ. Over the years I have noted a change in the way people relate to the idea of God. On the Alpha course we run at Holy Trinity Brompton, I've seen that people are quite happy to believe in 'God', which can mean anything. They can even believe in the Holy Spirit, which also could mean anything to them. The stumbling block is in coming to believe that Jesus is the unique Christ, the son of the living God.

It is important to focus on Jesus and not the devil. Father Raniero once said, 'To see the devil everywhere is no less a deviation from the truth, than to see him nowhere'.[1] Nowadays – and this is especially true of people outside the church – there seems to be as much superstition about demons and the devil as there was in the Middle Ages. You only have to look at the books that are published and the films that are made today. In the church, too, it can be tempting to see the devil everywhere, and even to go looking for demons. But Jesus never did that. He dealt with demons when they confronted him, but he never went looking for them.

We should not focus on the devil, and we should not focus too much on ourselves. The temptation is to be looking constantly within ourselves: 'Oh dear, I haven't done very well. Oh dear, I've failed again. Oh dear, I'm not a very good person.' Someone once said, 'Ten looks at him for one look within'. We must focus our attention on Jesus. When the temptation comes, we must fix our eyes on Jesus.

2. Keep short accounts

'Put on the breastplate of righteousness…'

(Ephesians 6:14).

Jesus died so that you and I could be righteous before God. This is what the cross achieved. God sees us as he sees his own son, Jesus; we, too, are totally

---

1 Fr Raniero Cantalamessa, *Come Creator Spirit: Meditations on the Veni Creator* (Protea Book House, 2003), p.295.

righteous in his sight. (Righteousness means to have a right relationship with God and with others.) Yet, we fall, we sin, we mess up. The key is to keep short accounts when we fall. First of all, short accounts with God. When we sin, the remedy is to say, 'Oh God, I am so sorry, I have done it again, please forgive me'. Rather than waiting, we should come back to God quickly.

Reading the questionnaires filled out at the end of an Alpha course, I sometimes read a comment like this: 'Twenty years ago I was a Christian, and then I messed up and I've been in the wilderness for twenty years. Ten weeks ago I walked into this church and I've come back to Christ.' Although of course I am delighted to hear of a relationship with God that has been restored, my response is, 'Do not wait twenty years, or even twenty minutes'. We can come back straight away. It is key to close the gap between when we fall and when we come back.

It is important that we do not become isolated; we all struggle and we need to share in those struggles. Unforgiveness blocks our relationship with others and thereby it blocks our relationship with God.

R. T. Kendall was the pastor of Westminster Chapel. I once heard him say:

Sometime after I became a minister in London, one Saturday morning I started my preparation for my Sunday sermon. Normally at Westminster Chapel I'd start my preparation for the Sunday on the Monday before, and have a whole week. But it had been a very busy week and I had been all over Britain preaching and I didn't even have time to look at one book, I didn't have time to look at the Greek. But I thought, 'Well I've got Saturday'. At nine o'clock that morning, just before I sat down to prepare, [my wife] Louise and I got into an argument in the kitchen. Let's just say it was a dandy. She was horrible. I went to my chair, sat down, opened my Bible, got out some paper and a pen, and prayed, 'Jesus help me, Lord, I need your word today, deal with that woman!' It was eleven o' clock, I had nothing. 'Lord I really need your help. Jesus, please help me, give me some thoughts here.' One o'clock, nothing. I prayed again, 'Lord please. Everything I say tomorrow is going to be tape recorded. It's going to go around the world, and you have got to help me.' It was as if God looked down and said, 'Really?' I said, 'Lord, I've got to have help'. Three o'clock. Nothing. Four o'clock.

Now it had crossed my mind at nine o'clock, but I was waiting for her. Finally God knew how to deal with me, and I went to her on bended knee, and I said, 'I am sorry, it is my fault'. She said, 'Well it was not all your fault, it was partly my fault'. I said, 'No, it was all my fault, totally my fault'. We hugged, we kissed. I went back to the same chair, opened the Bible, and I promise you, in forty five minutes I had everything I needed for Sunday morning.

As soon as he asked his wife for forgiveness, his relationship with God was restored. We must keep short accounts.

3. Get actively involved

'… with your feet fitted with the readiness that comes from the gospel of peace'

(Ephesians 6:15).

Where we take our feet is hugely important. If you are struggling with alcoholism, do not go into a pub to try out the peanuts. Paul tells of 'Feet fitted with the readiness that comes from the gospel of peace'. The devil hates the Gospel, because the Gospel is the power of God to change people's lives.

I love being involved in a small group on the Alpha course, because in the small group you observe the power of the Gospel to change people's lives.

I met Pete Dobbs, 44, from South London, on our Alpha course at Holy Trinity Brompton.

Pete grew up on a council estate; his father died when he was fifteen. He was a Chelsea supporter and became a football hooligan in his late teens. He said:

We'd fight against West Ham, Millwall, Cardiff – it didn't matter who it was. Sometimes we'd go into a pub and smash it up – picking up chairs, ramming them through the windows, just causing trouble. We'd fight until we got dispersed by the police.

He spent time in prison for burglary and got involved with the National Front, beating up foreigners. A member of the infamous 'Chelsea Headhunters', he enjoyed his reputation as a violent man and was once hired to kill someone. He said, 'I used to enjoy beating people up. I was a stressed and angry person.'

Pete came on Alpha and he said this:

> Basically, one day I found the Lord, or I should say, the Lord found me. The Lord has changed my life. I don't get angry and I don't get stressed, I just love everybody and I can't do enough for anybody. It's amazing what the Lord has done and I'm just so pleased that the he has saved my life. The old Peter Dobbs is dead and here is the new Peter Dobbs! After the Alpha weekend I woke up and I knew that the Lord had told me 'Pete, you're going to go to Africa and you're going to go and build some houses and schools,' because I'm a builder. So very soon, I'm going to be off to Africa to build some houses.

That is the power of God to change people's lives – a man who was involved in the National Front going to Africa to build houses and schools.

That is why we need to be active in struggling against temptation. John Wimber used to say, 'It is hard to sit still and be good'. We need to be actively involved in the Christian life. Whether we are working with the poor, the broken, or in the prisons, when we serve we can see God changing lives through the power of the Gospel.

4. Trust God in difficult times

'In addition to all this, take up the shield of faith, with which you can extinguish all the flaming arrows of the evil one' (Ephesians 6:16).

'Arrows' refers to things such as false guilt, doubt, disobedience, lust, malice and fear. Perhaps you have noticed that the devil chooses to attack us when we are at our most vulnerable. I heard of a helpful acrostic: the times when we're most vulnerable make up the word HALT. We are at our most vulnerable to temptation when we are **H**ungry (either physically or spiritually), **A**nxious, **L**onely, or **T**ired. At those moments we must take up the shield of faith. However, there are times when we are under a prolonged attack. Paul writes about 'the day of evil'. There are times when a spiritual attack goes on for weeks, months or even years. Mother Teresa's diaries, found after she died, revealed how she went through what she described as 'the dark night of the soul'. For most of her life, although outwardly she was serving the Lord, inwardly she was struggling.

There have been times in my life where I have felt under attack for a prolonged period. Just before I went to theological college I felt that the power of temptation was very strong. Martin Luther said, 'The power of temptation stupefies'. There was a moment at that time when the temptation was unbelievably powerful; it stupefied. There followed a period of sickness, my wife Pippa and I were ill for about a year with hepatitis. The sickness was followed by an intellectual attack. I began to read attacks on Christianity from some very intelligent people who knew the Bible well. This began to chip away at my faith and I became disillusioned by theological college. I used to go to chapel and think, 'Is this what people are being taught to do when they go to their churches, because if it is then I don't think anyone's going to come'. I wondered, 'What am I getting myself involved in, why am I doing this? Why did I stop being a barrister?' It was so much more fun being a barrister. After theological college I tried to get a job, and could not find a position anywhere. After that there were financial problems, then family rows, and then my mother died quite suddenly of a heart attack. I started to dread the 'phone ringing, because I knew that it would bring more bad news. My prayers did not seem to be answered. I thought it would never end. But by God's grace, the time of suffering did come to an end.

There are periods in all of our lives when all we can do is hang on to the shield of faith and say, 'I don't feel anything, I'm not experiencing your presence Lord, but I know you are real, and I'm going to keep on believing. Not because of the evidence, but in spite of the evidence to the contrary.' At these times we must take the shield of faith, with which we can extinguish all the flaming arrows of the evil one.

5. Guard your mind

'Take the helmet of salvation…'   *(Ephesians 6:17).*

Bishop B. F. Westcott, who was Regius professor of Divinity at Cambridge University, was once asked by a rather zealous member of the Christian Union, 'Bishop, are you saved?' His response was this, 'A very good question, but tell me, do you mean…'. He went on to mention three passive participles of the Greek verb 'to save', indicating that his answer would depend on which of the three the student had in mind. He said, 'I know I have *been* saved, I believe I'm *being* saved, and I hope by the grace of God that I *shall* be saved'. In other words we have been set free (which is another term for save). We *have been* set free from the *penalty* of sin; this is the past. We know that we are totally forgiven. Right now, we struggle with the *power* of sin, but we are being set free from it. One day we will be set free from the *presence* of sin, as there will be no temptation at all in heaven. The future is secure, but right now we struggle, and the battle starts in the mind. That is why Paul talks of the 'helmet of salvation', because every temptation starts in the mind.

I once spoke to a youth pastor who told me that he found he was at his most vulnerable when he returned home from a particularly rewarding teaching session with his youth group. He often found it difficult to wind down after these events and, once home, would flick through the television channels to try and relax. He came across programmes he knew he probably shouldn't watch because of their content – perhaps they were overly sexual, or featured half-naked or naked people – and this was one of the areas where he felt at his most tempted. He really struggled with this until he realised he had a great home group, and particularly a great group of men, whom he could turn to for guidance. Once he had talked honestly and openly to the men in the group he found he had a support network that he could turn to when he was struggling. They now have an arrangement whereby, if any one of them is battling temptation, they can call each other, day or night. He now actively encourages anyone who is dealing with any kind of temptation to talk frankly to their Christian friends. This youth pastor demonstrated a determination to win the battle of the mind. We have to guard what we think about.

6. Soak yourself in the word of God

'Take the sword of the spirit, which is the
word of God'   *(Ephesians 6:17).*

The collect in *The Book of Common Prayer* on the second Sunday in Advent says that we should hear the word of God and then we should 'read, mark, learn and inwardly digest it'. The Bible is the main way in which we hear God's voice and we must listen to his voice every day. Of course we hear God's voice through the gifts of the Spirit – through prophecy, through tongues and interpretation, through worship and through prayer. Supremely, however, we hear God's voice through the word of God in the Bible. This is why I encourage you to soak yourself in it. Rick Warren said:

In the second year of this church [Saddleback, California, USA], I went through a period of major depression. I had some physical problems at the beginning of the year and it got me depressed, no energy. There was so much to be done and it just depressed me. I was under a cloud for most of the first part of that year. I was so discouraged and so depressed. What I did is I got these little white cards. On one side of the card I would write a positive scripture verse. On the back I'd write a practical application of the verse, for me in the form of a personal affirmation. So, I'd write the verse, 'There is therefore no condemnation for those in Christ'. I'd turn it over and I'd write, 'God does not condemn me for my depression. He loves me, just as much on my bad days as on my good days.' On another card I wrote down, 'I can do all things through Christ who strengthens me'. On the back I'd write, 'I can make it through this day, in fact it's going to be better than yesterday. I'm getting stronger.' I don't know if I'll ever get over this depression, I was worried about that, but I'm not afraid of depression. Why? Take another card, 'There is no fear in love, perfect love casts out all fear'. I wrote these things down, I had a whole stack of them. Every night as I went to bed, the last thing I did was to read those verses, those affirmations, think about them. When I woke up, before I got out of bed, I'd pull them over, I'd read them. I'd put them in my pocket, carry them with me and began to reprogramme my mind, thinking positive thoughts and creating new ruts in my mind. In about four or five weeks, that massive depression just lifted. I want to tell you from personal experience, I don't get depressed anymore. Everybody gets discouraged, but I don't battle massive depression. Why? Because I reprogrammed my mind. People say, 'Why are you such a positive person?' I train myself. I memorize the truth about life from the Bible, rather than believe in the lies about life from the TV news and from what other people were saying. It has been a major shift.

Paul says, 'Be strong in the Lord, and in his [Jesus'] mighty power'. 'Put on the armour of God [the Father].' 'Pray' in the Holy Spirit. The whole Trinity is on our side. We need the whole Trinity because the stakes are high and there is a war on.

Conclusion

We are called to play our part. We are called to stand against the enemy in the power of Jesus Christ, and to say 'no' to all forms of temptation and evil. If we stand against the enemy and do everything we can to ensure that we, individually and as a church, are strong in the Lord and in his mighty power, we will see the name of Jesus honoured again in our country.

If you would like to find out more about the Alpha course and its related ministries, please see **alpha.org**

Also by Nicky Gumbel:

Is God a Delusion?

Drawing upon his experience as a barrister, Nicky Gumbel addresses the biggest issue of our age: does God exist?

(Book / Code 9781905887194 / £4.99)

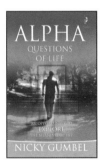

Alpha - Questions of Life

The Alpha course talks in book form. Over 1.3 million copies sold.

(Book / Code HTB04 /
Trade Code 9781842911648 / £6.99)

Searching Issues

Tackles the seven most common objections to the Christian faith.

(Book / Code HTB05 /
Trade Code 9780854767397 / £6.99)

Challenging Lifestyle

Examines the Sermon on the Mount and presents us with some radical alternatives for how to live in the 21st century. A small group DVD and manuals for guests also available.

(Book / Code HTB46 /
Trade Code 9780854767427 / £6.99)

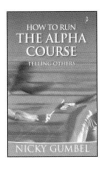

How to Run The Alpha Course - Telling Others

A useful 'how to' book that includes material from the Alpha conference and Alpha leaders' training.

(Book / Code HTB20 /
Trade Code 9781842911723 / £6.99)

30 Days

An excellent introduction to reading the Bible, designed to be read over thirty days.

(Booklet / Code 9781902750811 / £2.50)

A Life Worth Living

Based on Paul's letter to the Philippians, this book offers a practical and positive guide to achieving exactly this.

(Book/Code HTB09/Trade Code 9780854767403/£6.99)

Why Jesus?

An evangelistic booklet for those having their first thoughts about the Christian faith. Designed to be given away.

Christmas and Easter versions of *Why Jesus?* are also available, see alphashop.org for more details.

(Booklet/Code 9781904074571/£0.50 Large Print Booklet/Code 9781905887156/£0.50)

Other titles from Nicky Gumbel available from alphashop.org

Alpha

Available to order from your local Christian bookshop, or from: **www.alphashop.org**

Phone the Alpha Publications Hotline on **0845 758 1278** or **email alpha@stl.org**
To order from overseas: **+44 1228 611749**